China

Janet Riehecky

Carolrhoda Books, Inc. / Minneapolis

Photo Acknowledgments

Photos, maps, and artworks are used courtesy of: John Erste, pp. 1, 2–3, 18–19, 23, 25 (top), 29, 33, 39, 40–41, 41; Laura Westlund, pp. 4–5, 21; © Wolfgang Kaehler, pp. 6 (top), 8, 9, 11, 13, 14 (bottom), 16, 17 (both), 18 (left), 20, 22, 26, 30 (left), 37, 43 (top); © Eugene G. Schulz, pp. 6 (bottom), 15, 21, 24, 31, 40; Visuals Unlimited: (© Charles Preitner) p. 7, (© Jeff Greenberg) p. 14 (top), (© Steve McCutcheon) p. 18 (right), (© Jon Turk) p. 19, (© Will Trover) pp. 30 (right), 44, (© Robin Karpan) p. 34 (bottom), (© N. Pecnic) p. 39, (© Fritz Pölking) p. 45; ChinaStock: (© Dennis Cox) p. 10 (left), (© Liu Xiaoyang) p. 28, (© Christopher Liu) pp. 29, 32, 36, 38; © Brian A. Vikander, pp. 10 (right), 34 (top), 35 (bottom); Robert Fried Photography: (© Robert Fried) p. 12, (© Sophie Dauwe) pp. 27, 43 (bottom); Lejla Fazlic Omerovic, p. 25 (bottom); F. Botts/FAO, p. 35 (top); © Michele Burgess, p. 42. Cover photo of detail of Nine-Dragon Wall © Wolfgang Kaehler.

Contents

Huanying ni dao Zhongguo lai!*

*That's "Welcome to China" in Chinese, the official language of China.

 China, the world's third-largest nation in size, covers 3.7 million square miles. Only Russia and Canada are bigger. China dominates Asia, the biggest continent in the world.

China shares its eastern border with the Pacific Ocean. The part of the Pacific that touches China is divided into three seas. It's probably no surprise that the East China Sea is to the east and the South China Sea is to the south. The Yellow Sea touches China's northeastern shore. To the south lie thick forests and more of the Pacific Ocean.

Mountains and **deserts** separate China from countries to the north, southwest, and west. China's borders meet those of 14 other countries. Can you find them on the map?

China is divided into 22 provinces (states). The country also has three municipalities (cities so big that they are like provinces). China's five autonomous regions are like provinces, except that they govern themselves.

KAZAKHSTAN

KYRGYZSTAN

TAJIKISTAN

AFGHANISTAN

PAKISTAN

TIAN SHAN

Turpan Depression —

TARIM BASIN

XINJIANG

TAKLIMAKAN DESERT

C

KUNLUN SHAN

GANGDÎSE

TIBET

HIMALAYAS

INDIA

NEPAL

Mount Everest

BHUTAN

INDIAN OCEAN

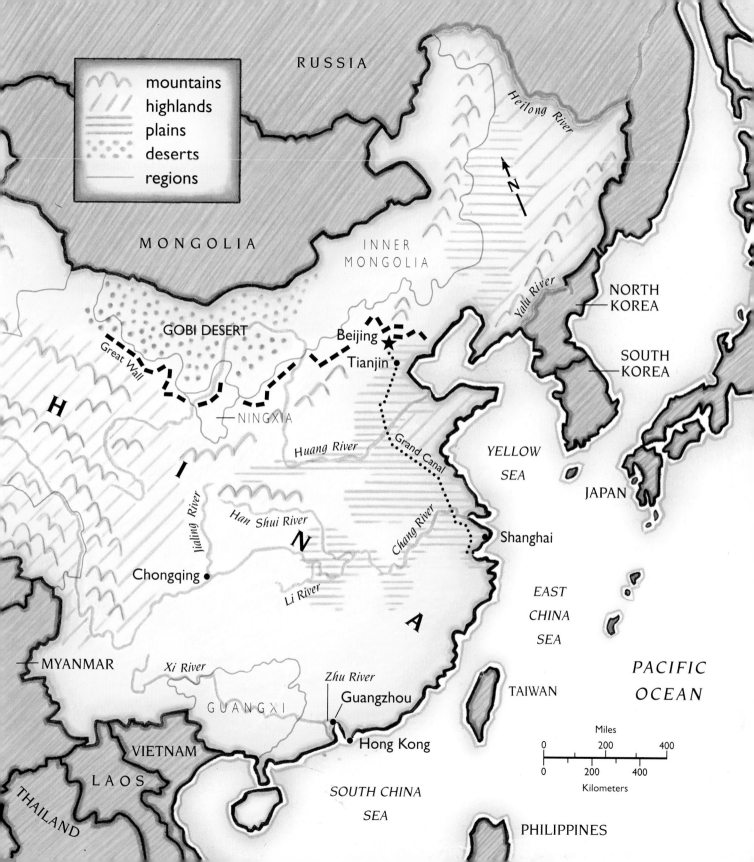

Three Steps **Up**

China's landscape looks like three steps of a giant staircase. The lowest step is eastern China. This area has broad valleys, grassy **plains,** rolling hills, and many rivers. The land is good to farm, and the weather does not get uncomfortably hot or bitterly cold. No surprise! Almost everyone in China lives on the lowest step.

Fields and trees dot a small town near the Turpan Depression.

Rice paddies (fields) cover much of eastern China. People have cut into hills to make more rice paddies.

The second, higher step makes up the middle part of China. Here the land is a mixture of mountains, **basins,** and **plateaus.** Basins sink into the ground. The lowest point in China, the Turpan Depression, is part of the Tarim Basin in western China. Plateaus are large, raised, flat areas found in mountain ranges. They look like mountains with the tops cut off.

Fast Facts

Name: People's Republic of China (PRC)

Area: 3.7 million square miles

Main Landforms: Himalaya Mountains, Kunlun Shan, Tian Shan, Gobi Desert, Taklimakan Desert, Tarim Basin

Rivers: Huang River, Chang River, Xi River, Li River

Highest Point: Mount Everest (29,028 feet high)

Lowest Point: Turpan Depression (465 feet below sea level)

Animals: Giant panda, white-lipped deer, Chinese river dolphin, Yangtze alligator

Capital City: Beijing

Other Major Cities: Tianjin, Shanghai, Hong Kong

Official Language: Putongua

Money Unit: Yuan

The huge, western part of China—the third step—is made up of towering mountains and high, cold plateaus. The winters are long and very chilly, so not many people live in this area. The Himalaya Mountains jut into the sky. One Himalayan peak, Mount Everest (known in China as Qomolungma), is the tallest mountain in the world. It sits on the border of the country of Nepal and the Tibet autonomous region. Other mountain ranges, such as the Tian Shan and the Kunlun Shan, are scattered throughout the western part of China.

The high, rugged peaks of the Himalayas (right) reach into the sky of Tibet in western China. Tibet is nicknamed "the roof of the world" because it's so high.

Two men steer their boat up the Grand Canal, the longest waterway ever made. The Chinese began building the canal in the A.D. 400s. They didn't use modern machines. They dug the canal by hand!

Water You Going
to Do?

Imagine stepping out your front door right into a boat! It's not a raging flood. It's everyday life in southern China's water villages. Houses hug the banks of streams and rivers. People take boat rides to visit family and friends or to go shopping.

China's rivers help people to travel, to transport their goods, and to **irrigate** (water) their crops. The country has three major rivers—the Chang in the middle, the Xi in the south, and the Huang in the north. The Chang, which runs from western China eastward to the Pacific Ocean, is the third-longest river in the world! The Xi River empties into the South China Sea.

The Huang follows a curving course from central China to the Pacific Ocean and irrigates much of northern China's cropland. But water doesn't always help. The Huang is nicknamed China's Sorrow because its floods have killed many people.

The Huang is sometimes called the Yellow River because of its color. During dry times, winds blow **loess** (a yellowish soil) off the ground and up into the air. When it rains, loess particles fall into the river, making the water look yellow. The Huang flows into the Yellow Sea and—guess what—turns its water yellow.

Some parts of China suffer from a lack of water. The northern and northwestern sections of China are extremely dry, especially the Gobi and the Taklimakan Deserts.

The Great Green Wall

When fierce winds blow loess from farmland, crops no longer have good soil to grow in. Healthy farmland can be turned into a bare, windy desert. Chinese scientists decided to try and stop the desert by building a barrier made of trees planted close together. The trees' roots might hold the soil in place. The scientists hope the wall will keep the desert from spreading.

People of China

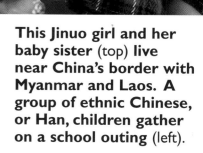

Most Chinese people—about 92 percent—are **ethnic Chinese** (sometimes called the Han **ethnic group).** An ethnic group is made up of people who share beliefs, customs, and a single history. The ethnic Chinese speak Chinese.

This Jinuo girl and her baby sister (top) **live near China's border with Myanmar and Laos. A group of ethnic Chinese, or Han, children gather on a school outing** (left).

Wearing a traditional outfit, a Hua Yao Dai woman from southern China spins wool into yarn.

Women Hold Up Half the Sky

Posters and billboards in China proclaim that "women hold up half the sky." The Chinese government puts up these signs to remind people that women are just as important as men. At one time in China's history, women were treated like property. These days men and women have equal rights.

Members of 55 other ethnic groups make their homes in China, and most live near the country's borders. People of these groups might not speak Chinese. They use their own languages and live the way their **ancestors** did thousands of years ago.

Sometimes it's hard for people with different languages and customs to get along. But the Chinese work at being friends with one another. An important part of Chinese culture is cooperation. Chinese law also requires that everyone be treated equally.

Three Is a
Family

A typical family of three strolls through their hometown of Shanghai.

In past times, Chinese **extended families** liked to live together in one big house. Most homes included grandparents, parents, and lots and lots of kids. In those days, families had many children.

These days most households are made up of parents and children. Grandparents, aunts, uncles, and cousins might live nearby. But the biggest change in the Chinese family is that most parents only have one kid.

China has more people than any other country—more than 1.2 billion—and the population will probably keep getting bigger. One of every five people on our planet lives in China! About 28 percent of the Chinese are under the age of 15. When these young folks grow up and have children of their own, even more people will live in China.

It is hard to feed, house, and care for so many people. The Chinese are trying to slow population growth in their country. The government gives bonuses and special privileges to families with only one kid. It punishes couples with two or more kids by charging fines. These efforts have helped, but China still faces overpopulation problems.

All in the Family

Here are the Chinese words for family members. Practice using these terms on your own family. See if they can understand you!

grandfather	*zufu*	(dzoo-foo)
grandmother	*zumu*	(dzoo-moo)
father	*fuqin*	(foo-chihn)
mother	*muqin*	(moo-chihn)
uncle	*shushu*	(shoo-shoo)
aunt	*ayi*	(ah-ee)
son	*er.zi*	(ER-dzeh)
daughter	*nuer*	(noo-er)
older brother	*ge.ge*	(GUH-guh)
younger brother	*de.de*	(DEE-dee)
older sister	*jie.jie*	(JEE-EH-jee-eh)
younger sister	*mei.mei*	(MAY-may)

Big **Cities**

Shoppers and traffic bustle in Shanghai, China's biggest city (left). **Many people can squeeze into these huge apartment buildings in Hong Kong** (below).

China boasts some of the world's biggest cities. Tianjin, Shanghai, and Beijing (the capital) are so big that they are municipalities. Remember that word?

More than 11 million people live in Beijing. Universities, museums, ancient palaces, and government offices make Beijing a center of activity.

Hong Kong

In the 1800s, European governments were at war with China's rulers over trading rights. As a reward for winning one of the wars, Great Britain got Hong Kong Island, which sits off China's coast in the South China Sea. Later Great Britain came to control many small islands and a little bit of the mainland. This area is called Hong Kong. Over the years, Hong Kong grew into a trade center. Hong Kong's more than 6 million people own businesses that make goods sold across the world. But Hong Kong remained a British possession, and China wanted it back. After many meetings, Great Britain agreed to return Hong

Kong to China in 1997. These days the Zhu River (part of the Xi River) brings trade goods and people from the bustling Chinese city of Guangzhou to the Hong Kong region. Hong Kong is again an important part of China!

Beijing is crowded, but even more people—more than 13 million—live in Shanghai! This city is a good place to do business, and many Chinese come to Shanghai looking for jobs. Other Chinese cities—such as Tianjin and Guangzhou—also have huge populations.

Lots of people means there isn't room to spread out. Roads are jammed. Almost everyone in Chinese cities lives in cramped apartments, but some people have small houses in older neighborhoods. The cities are so packed that two families might share one little apartment!

At Home on the Farm

Although Chinese cities are crowded, most Chinese—about 75 percent—live in the country. Villages cluster around rivers and streams, often near good farmland. Most houses are made of stones or bricks.

While the kids go to school, most parents farm the land. In central and southeastern China, folks use water buffalo to pull plows and carts. In northeastern China, people grow wheat and use cattle to help out. Farmers irrigate fields and gardens from local waterways.

In China the government owns all the land and rents it to farmers. Most Chinese farmers belong to production teams, which are often

A farmer and his water buffalo plow a flooded rice paddy. These wet fields provide a lot of rice for Chinese people to eat.

made up of extended families. Each team plants and harvests a certain amount of food that goes to the government as rent. The government uses this food to feed China's huge population at a low cost. Farmers can keep or sell any extra food they produce. Some bring their freshest produce to open-air markets in big towns and cities, where people who don't grow their own food buy the goods.

Knee-deep in water, women plant a crop of rice (above). **A buyer and seller haggle over vegetables at an open-air market** (left).

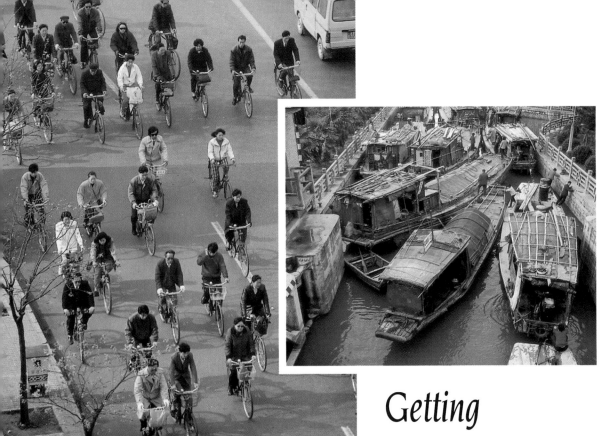

Bicycle commuters pedal by the thousands through Beijing's streets at morning rush hour (above). **A crowd of boats—some motorized, but most powered by people—jams the Grand Canal** (above right).

Getting
Around

Beijing has been called the city of 11 million people and 7 million bicycles. In China, many people ride their bikes to work, to the store, or to visit friends. Bike lanes keep riders safe from cars and buses. Folks in big cities might wait in long lines to catch buses. Almost no Chinese own cars.

Trains carry people on long journeys between major cities and into remote regions. In the countryside, many people use pack animals to move around. Some sail, paddle, or power along China's many waterways.

For China's nomads—most of whom belong to minority ethnic groups—travel is a way of life. Nomads move most of the year, stopping only at temporary camps. Nomadic peoples have roamed across northern and western regions of China for thousands of years. How do they go? On horseback, on camel, or even on foot.

The homes, called *gers*, of these northern Chinese nomads are made of heavy felt. People can take their gers apart and load them onto yak-drawn carts for traveling.

19

Historically Speaking . . .

China is one of the first places where people lived in permanent villages. People started farming in China about 150,000 years ago! More than 3,500 years ago, powerful rulers known as emperors began to run China.

Under the emperors, a few people were very rich, but high rents and high taxes kept most people poor. The common people grew angry about the way that the ruling class treated them.

In 1911 the Chinese rebelled against the emperor. But what kind of government should take the emperor's place? For more than 35 years, different groups fought to gain control of China. In 1949 the Chinese Communist Party, led by Mao Zedong, won. He formed the People's Republic of China (PRC).

Since then the PRC government has made sure that people have basic necessities such as food, schools, homes, and medical care. Most

An Astonishing Achievement

More than 2,000 years ago, the Chinese began building the Great Wall to keep out enemies. Although in most places the wall stands only about 25 feet high, it stretches almost 4,000 miles from the province of Inner Mongolia to the Pacific coast.

Centuries ago a Chinese emperor built the Imperial Palace. These days the palace bears a portrait of Mao Zedong.

families have enough money to buy things like bicycles, radios, and sewing machines. Many have electricity and telephone service. But there is a downside, too.

The PRC government tells most people where to live and what job to take. It punishes people who disagree with its policies. Most people don't have a chance to make very much money and can vote for only some PRC leaders.

Dear Grandpa,

Today I visited the Imperial Palace. It's nicknamed the Forbidden City because the emperor allowed only his family and his assistants inside. Luckily, it's no longer forbidden—in fact, 10,000 tourists a day visit the site!

I saw the Throne Hall, where the emperor once sat on a golden throne. Most of the palace is turned into museums full of Chinese art and cool old stuff! I saw a suit made of green jade, a kind of stone. A Chinese prince was buried in this suit more than 2,000 years ago. What a great day!

Love,
Teddy

Sun
Wam
Thalu
730

The Common
Language

Most people in China speak Chinese, but not all speak it the same way. In fact, folks in southern China speak a kind of Chinese that a person from the north might not understand!

China's official language is sometimes called Mandarin.

Two fabric merchants chat during a slow time at the market.

An Ancient Chinese Proverb

If you want happiness for an hour,
   take a nap.
If you want happiness for a day,
   go fishing.
If you want happiness for a month,
   get married.
If you want happiness for a year,
   inherit a fortune.
If you want happiness for a
   lifetime, help someone else.

The PRC government decided that everyone in China should be able to use the same version of Chinese. Officials chose the form of Chinese spoken in Beijing to be the common (shared) language, called *putongua*. Chinese kids learn putongua in school.

In Chinese a word gets its meaning not only from its sound, but also from the speaker's tone of voice. The spoken word *ma*, for example, can mean mother, horse, grasshopper, or to scold—depending on whether a person's voice goes up, dips down and then up, stays level, or falls.

An elementary student practices her writing. Chinese writing is an art form. People study for decades to make the elegant brush strokes of each character.

Some Real
Characters

Chinese does not have an alphabet. Instead, each word is represented by a symbol called a **character.** There are more than 50,000 characters for Chinese words!

Chinese kids have memorized the 2,000 most-often-used characters by the fourth grade. This number is enough to read a newspaper and many books. By the seventh grade, most students have mastered 3,000 characters. To enter college, a student has to know between 4,000 and 5,000 characters.

In the 1950s, the Chinese created pinyin—a way to write Chinese with the alphabet that English uses. Some students find pinyin easier to learn than characters.

Pinyin changed the way non-Chinese people spell Chinese words. The Chang River used to be written as the Yangtze River. Beijing used to be Peking. The spoken word is still the same—it's just the spelling that's changed. Some maps are still labeled with the old spellings.

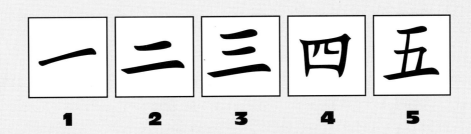

一	二	三	四	五
1	2	3	4	5

Calligraphy

The careful drawing, or calligraphy, of Chinese characters is an important art in China. The Chinese use bamboo brushes, black ink, and thin, white paper. Calligraphers create each stroke with special care—some thick, some thin. Try your hand at writing the numbers from one to five in Chinese.

A grandmother holds her baby granddaughter. If you visit China, someone might ask you how old you are. If you are older, the Chinese person might show extra respect to you. If you are younger, you would be expected to show extra respect.

Values and
Beliefs

In China people learn early to respect their parents and their ancestors. In past times, even grown-ups were supposed to obey *their* parents! These days adults make their own choices, but many still listen to their parents' opinions. Older people are considered wise and experienced, and younger people hope to learn from them.

Chinese culture values sharing, cooperation, and hard work. This culture has been influenced by three belief systems—Confucianism, Taoism, and Buddhism. Confucianism prizes a strict social order, respect for elders and for people in charge, and good manners. Taoism helps people learn to live in balance with nature. Buddhism teaches kindness and understanding. Buddhists often exhibit statues of the Buddha, the religion's founder. Even though only about 30 percent of Chinese people consider themselves religious, these belief systems have shaped Chinese thinking.

The Biggest Buddha in the World

Can you imagine a statue so big that 100 people could stand on one of its feet? The Leshan Buddha—the largest statue of the Buddha in the world—towers 213 feet over a place where three rivers join in south central China. A Buddhist monk began carving it in A.D. 713, and workers finished it almost 100 years later. Two people can stand up next to one another in each ear or sit, side by side, on a single toenail!

Celebrate!

Chinese New Year, or the Spring Festival, usually falls in late January. Before the celebration, people clean and decorate their homes. No one wants to dust, mop, or wipe away any new year luck, so people don't do any cleaning during the holiday. Everyone buys new clothes, pays old debts, and settles their fights. People put pieces of paper with good-luck sayings on walls, doors, and windows. They want a fresh start in the new year!

The new year's celebration usually lasts three days. A family dinner is an important part of the celebration. People cram the streets to watch outdoor gymnastics contests, dance performances, and parades. Parades begin with a huge paper lion whose movements scare away bad spirits. At the end, a long paper dragon appears. In Chinese legends, the dragon is a wise and helpful water god who brings rain and good luck.

Following the dragon's head, a line of drummers forms the scaly body in a Chinese New Year parade.

Costumed performers walk on stilts to entertain a crowd of Chinese New Year revelers.

Animal Years

Why is Chinese New Year at the *end* of January, instead of at the beginning as in other countries? China once followed a lunar (moon-based) calendar. This lunar year began on the first new moon after January 21. Eventually, the Chinese decided to follow the calendar that European and North American countries use, but the new year's celebration (now officially called the Spring Festival) stayed put.

There were 12 years in the old calendar, each named after an animal. Many different tales tell why the years are known by animal names. In one story, a wise emperor decides to hold a race for all animals. The animals run, hop, and flap along, arriving one after another at the emperor's feet. The emperor then names the years after the first 12 animals to finish the race.

School **Days**

Chinese students roll their eyes to the tune of a song. No kidding! In addition to stretching their arms and legs, students in China do exercises to prevent eye strain.

(Left) **Kindergarteners follow their teacher's lead, pretending to be monkeys during a midday play break.**

(Left) **Before their day begins, these schoolchildren do some eye exercises.**

Most Chinese kids go to school from age 6 to about age 12. They study reading, writing, math, science, music, and art. Because of shortages of teachers, buildings, and equipment, some classes have 60 students! That's a lot of kids. Co-operating and sharing are important parts of the school day in China.

School isn't just a place to study. Students spend part of the day cleaning the school, inside and out. Lots of schools have gardens, where students learn how to grow vegetables. A harvest might be part of the school lunch! Some schools also have a labor class once a week. Students might carry rocks from a quarry to a construction site or help to build a wall. The students, glad to help their community, don't mind the work.

Children's Palaces

In many cities, Children's Palaces provide after-school activities. The kids can play musical instruments, make puppets, paint, perform songs and dances, play games, or do science experiments.

Not all kids can go to Children's Palaces. Only students who work hard and do well in school are allowed. It's a special privilege.

Novels and
Folktales

Throughout their long history, the Chinese have written remarkable poems and stories. One of the best-loved tales is the *Romance of the Three Kingdoms* by Lo Guanzhong, written almost 1,500 years ago. This thrilling story about three rival kings in ancient China is still so popular that it was made into a video game. Maybe you've played it!

An illustration on an ancient manuscript shows a scene from the *Romance of the Three Kingdoms*.

A folktale is an old story that people pass down by word of mouth.

The Chinese also have many folktales that tell of magical treasures and deeds of bravery. The stories almost always teach an important lesson. One tells the story of Ye Shen, a young woman whose stepmother forces her to do all the housework. When her wicked stepmother kills Ye Shen's pet fish, the girl is heartbroken, but she soon discovers that the bones of the fish can grant wishes.

When everyone in the town goes to a festival, Ye Shen wishes that she could go, too. The bones give her such beautiful clothes and slippers that the king falls in love with her. When Ye Shen leaves before the king can learn her name, he is left with only one tiny slipper. . . . Does this story sound familiar? It's very similar to Cinderella, but it was written about a thousand years earlier.

What to **Wear?**

In the old days in China, it was sometimes easy to tell what social group a person was from. You could just look at their clothes! The rich often dressed in silk robes decorated with colorful stitching. Scholars were known by their blue robes. Most farmers wore straw hats and loose cotton pants and shirts.

During the reign of China's emperors, rich people wore beautiful silk robes (above). **Most farmers wore simple cotton clothing with straw hats** (left).

The Secret of Silk

Silk, among the richest fabrics in the world, was invented by the Chinese. Skilled workers make smooth, beautiful silk from the strands of fiber that the silkworm (a kind of caterpillar) uses to spin its cocoon. People figured out how to weave silk about 5,000 years ago, but the method was kept a carefully guarded secret for 3,000 years. No one is sure how other countries learned to make silk. One legend tells that a Chinese princess who married an Indian prince hid silkworm eggs in her headdress to share the secret. Another tale says that some Buddhist monks brought the silkworms to India.

In modern China, most kids wear the same kinds of clothes as in Europe or in North America. Military-style uniforms are common, too.

After the Communist Party came to power in 1949, everyone wore the same kind of clothes—dark-colored pants with a jacket and a small cap. In the 1970s, people began to dress with more variety, but the dark uniforms are still popular, as are loose-fitting pants and shirts. People in rural China usually aim for comfort instead of fashion. In cities some businesspeople choose business suits or dresses.

Table tennis is popular at this Beijing school. The playground has several permanent tables.

Games and
Leisure

"Cooperation first; competition second." That's a slogan often seen in China, where sports and games, such as volleyball and table tennis, are popular. Winning takes second place to building character. Fans watching a game don't root for just one team—they enjoy skillful play. Playing fair is also very important.

Teachers watch students carefully to see if any have a natural ability for sports, dance, or other athletic activities. A gifted student might attend one of the 3,000 schools where young athletes focus on perfecting their skills. Some Chinese Olympic champions got their starts at these talent schools.

Chinese towns are dotted with parks, where kids and adults fly kites, stroll, and picnic. In the morning, many Chinese do special exercises called *wushu*, or **martial arts.** They gracefully go through a series of movements that are useful for self-defense. Others exercise by practicing dances such as the tango.

People of all ages gather at a public square in Beijing to do their morning exercises together.

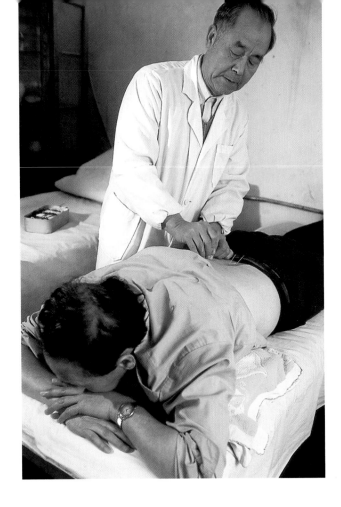

Doctors who perform acupuncture may insert the needles several inches deep! Even so, most patients say the treatment doesn't hurt at all.

Pins and
Needles

Do you think that sticking a long, thin needle into your skin could cure a headache? It might be a Chinese doctor's solution. This Chinese practice—called acupuncture—dates back 4,000 years. Of course, only highly skilled professionals can find the special places to insert the needles. Most patients don't even feel the prick. The Chinese believe that acupuncture can cure more than 100 diseases.

Other doctors in China use the latest high-tech methods. Many believe in **holistic medicine,** which treats a whole person, instead of just a disease or injury. These doctors think that a happy outlook on life is a good way to keep healthy.

Acupressure

Acupuncture should only be done by a doctor who knows how to perform it. But anyone can try acupressure! The next time you have a headache, try slowly pressing your fingertip on a point above your left eye, just where the eyebrow begins, next to your nose. Feel gently for a place where the skin seems to dip in slightly. Press gently but firmly for three to ten minutes, until the muscles relax. Release the pressure slowly. Is your headache gone?

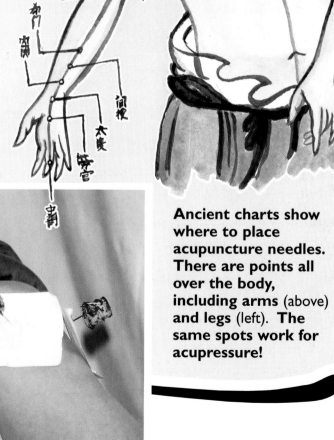

Ancient charts show where to place acupuncture needles. There are points all over the body, including arms (above) **and legs** (left). **The same spots work for acupressure!**

39

The Food of *China*

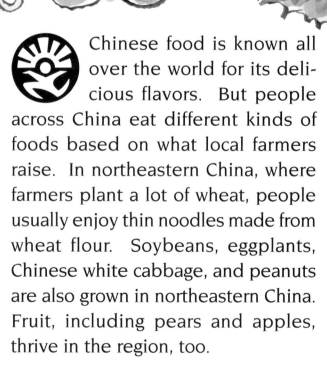

An open-air market in Shanghai offers all the ingredients for a delicious Chinese meal.

Chinese food is known all over the world for its delicious flavors. But people across China eat different kinds of foods based on what local farmers raise. In northeastern China, where farmers plant a lot of wheat, people usually enjoy thin noodles made from wheat flour. Soybeans, eggplants, Chinese white cabbage, and peanuts are also grown in northeastern China. Fruit, including pears and apples, thrive in the region, too.

The land around the Chang River, in central eastern China, is a good place to produce tea, pumpkins, and water lilies. Farmers cultivate rice on rice paddies. People in this area eat rice just about every day. The southern part of China, where the climate is warm and wet, often has three rice harvests a year! Bitter green melons, papayas, Chinese broccoli, and guavas all grow well in this climate.

Chinese people don't usually eat meat every day. When they do, chicken, duck, and pork are favorites.

Soy what?

One of the most important parts of Chinese cooking isn't rice or noodles. Soybeans—a Chinese favorite—are cheap and healthy. Cooking with them is easy. Chinese people use soybeans to make bean curd (known to some as tofu), which ranges from firm to silky smooth in texture. Soy sauce, a popular flavoring, comes from soybeans, flour, and water. Chili bean sauce is a blend of chilis, yellow soybeans, and seasonings. This spicy dark paste adds zest to many dishes. Other recipes call for black soybeans. Although most of the soybeans are grown in northeastern China, farmers raise the crop throughout eastern China.

M*mm,* **Good!**

A festive-looking noodle dish brightens the table at an outdoor restaurant.

Only about 10 percent of Chinese households have refrigerators. But Chinese cooks like ingredients to be very, very fresh. To get the freshest foods, some busy people shop at open-air markets early in the morning before they go to work. Some go to the market three times a day!

Cooks begin many Chinese dishes by chopping vegetables—like Chinese white cabbage, lettuce, and bean sprouts—into bite-size bits. They then stir-fry the vegetables by rapidly cooking them in oil in a sturdy skillet over a hot stove. Seasonings such as scallions, garlic, or ginger are added, too.

Balancing textures and flavors is important in Chinese cooking. Crunchy peanuts might be added to soft noodles. Sweet and sour is a popular combination of flavors. So is serving both cool and hot dishes.

Almost no one in China eats with a knife and a fork. Diners use chopsticks! Chopsticks are long, thin, wooden sticks held by the fingers of one hand. People use the sticks to grasp bits of food, as if the sticks were extra fingers.

A chef (above) **makes dumplings, a popular Chinese food. At a festival in southern China, kids use chopsticks to eat noodles** (right).

Glossary

ancestor: A relative from the past, such as one's great-great-great grandparent.

basin: A bowl-shaped region, often surrounded by highlands or mountains.

character: A graphic symbol used to represent a word or letter.

desert: A dry, sandy region that receives low amounts of rainfall.

ethnic Chinese: A descendant of an early people called the Han who make up the largest ethnic group in China.

ethnic group: A large community of people that shares a number of social features in common such as language, religion, or customs.

extended family: Mothers, fathers, brothers, sisters, grandparents, aunts, uncles, and cousins who may live together in one household.

holistic medicine: A way of practicing medicine that focuses on treating a person's state of mind and general well-being as well as specific ailments or injuries.

irrigate: To bring water to land so that crops can grow even if there is no rain.

About 2,200 years ago, a Chinese emperor prepared an army for his tomb! More than 8,000 life-size, clay warriors guard the grave.

loess: A yellowish soil that is good for growing crops. During dry times, strong winds can blow loess up into the air.

martial arts: Several types of combat and self-defense, such as karate, that were developed in China, Japan, and Korea.

plain: A broad, flat area of land that has few trees or other outstanding natural features.

plateau: A large area of high, level land.

Wild China

Many forests in China have been cut down to create more farmland. This loss of forests has caused problems for a favorite Chinese animal, the giant panda. In the wild, a giant panda eats only one kind of food—the leaves, stems, and shoots of the bamboo—and makes its home in the shrinking bamboo forests. The government has set up 13 panda reserves, but scientists worry that it may be too late for the pandas. Experts believe that fewer than 1,000 giant pandas live in the forests.

Pronunciation Guide*

autonomous region	aw-TAH-nah-muhs REE-jihn
Beijing	BAY-JING
guangxi	GWAHNG-SHEE
Huang	HOOAHNG
huanying ni dao zhongguo lai	hwan-yihng NEE DOW johng-guo LYE
Kunlun Shan	KWOON-LOON SHAHN
Laozi	LOW-DZEH
Li	LEE
Lo Guanzhong	LWOH guan-joong
Mao Zedong	MOW dzuh-DOONG
Qomolungma	kwoh-moh-loong-ma
Taklimakan	TAHK-lih-mahk-AHN
Tarim	TAH-RIM
Tian Shan	TEEAHN SHAHN
Tianjin	TEEAHN-JIHN
Turpan	toor-PAHN
Xi	SHEE
Ye Shen	YEH SHEN
Zhu	JOO

*Pronunciations are approximate.

Further Reading

China in Pictures. Minneapolis: Lerner Publications Company, 1988.

Louie, Ai-Ling. *Yeh-Shen: A Cinderella Story from China* (retold). New York: Philomel Books, 1982.

Mitchell, Barbara. *Between Two Worlds: A Story About Pearl Buck.* Minneapolis: Carolrhoda Books, 1988.

Pitkänen, Matti A. *The Children of China.* Minneapolis: Carolrhoda Books, 1990.

Scheider, Michal. *Between the Dragon and the Eagle.* Minneapolis: Carolrhoda Books, 1997.

Street Smart! Cities of the Ancient World. Minneapolis: Runestone Press, 1994.

Willcox, Isobel. *Acrobats & Ping-Pong: Young China's Games, Sports, and Amusements.* New York: Dodd, Mead & Company, 1981.

Yu, Ling. *Cooking the Chinese Way.* Minneapolis: Lerner Publications Company, 1982.

Metric Conversion Chart

WHEN YOU KNOW:	MULTIPLY BY:	TO FIND:
teaspoon	5.0	milliliters
Tablespoon	15.0	milliliters
cup	0.24	liters
inches	2.54	centimeters
feet	0.3048	meters
miles	1.609	kilometers
square miles	2.59	square kilometers
degrees Fahrenheit	5/9 (after subtracting 32)	degrees Celsius

Index

acupressure, 39
acupuncture, 38, 39

Beijing, 7, 14, 18, 25, 36, 37
bicycles, 18
Buddha, 27
Buddhism, 26, 27

characters, 24–25
Children's Palaces, 31
Chinese New Year, 28, 29
chopsticks, 43
cities, 14–15, 18
clothes, 11, 34–35
Communist Party, 20, 35
Confucianism, 26–27.

deserts, 4, 9
doctors, 38–39

emperors, 20, 29, 34, 44
ethnic groups, 10–11

faith, 26–27
families, 12–13
farmers, 6, 8–9, 16–17, 34,
    40, 41
food, 40–41, 42–43

government, 11, 13, 16–17,
    20–21, 23

Grand Canal, 8, 18
Great Wall, 20

history of China, 20–21
holidays, 28–29
Hong Kong, 15
houses, 8, 14, 15, 16, 19

Imperial Palace, 21

languages, 10–11, 13, 22–23,
    24–25
Laozi, 27

Mao Zedong, 20, 21
map of China, 4–5
markets, 17, 22, 40, 42
martial arts, 37
mountains, 4, 6, 7

nomads, 19

Pacific Ocean, 4, 8, 9
people, 10–11
People's Republic of China
    (PRC), 20–21, 23
pinyin, 24–25
plateaus, 6, 7
playtime, 36–37
respect, 26–27
rice paddies, 6, 16, 41

rivers, 8–9

schools, 23, 30–31
seas, 4, 9
Shanghai, 7, 12, 14, 15, 40
silk, 34, 35
soybeans, 41
stories, 32–33

Taoism, 26, 27
Tarim Basin, 6, 7
Tianjin, 7, 14
Tibet, 7
travel methods, 8, 18–19
trees and forests, 4, 9, 45
Turpan Depression, 6, 7

weather, 6, 7
women, 11